THE GREAT SHIFT

'explained'

The World You Have Known

Is Collapsing. Here Is Why It's a GIFT

John McIntosh

Published by ONE-SELF Productions

ISBN: 9798680617687

We gratefully acknowledge **Solveig Larsen** for
providing the image for the cover

INDEX

PREFACE

*You have been dreaming and the dream has been very deep and totally convincing ... so much so that everything that is happening in your world right now looks and feels very 'real'. Very, very few actually 'see' through this illusion but there is **a Great SHIFT** occurring now that will allow many more to see.*

This version of your dream world that you have called reality, is collapsing. For eons Life has been *upside down* ... an illusion so real that only a few down through the ages have recognized the Truth and set themselves Free. Humanity is now being **shaken awake** through this **Great SHIFT**.

This shaking is **fierce** and occurs through dramatic challenges, well beyond what most **can endure**. And yet, it is through suffering that the vast majority of humanity comes to its knees in **surrender** where the turn inward leads to the **Awareness of Who YOU Really Are.**

It matters NOT whether you believes in some powerful *source* outside yourself or in nothing at all. When one has reached their breaking point there is a *desperate hope* that *something* exists that can lift you from the depths of despair.

This brief eBook will explain *What* is happening, *Why* its an enormous *GIFT* and *How* to navigate this *Great SHIFT.*

CHAPTER ONE
REALITY

There **is** only **ONE**, which is boundless, timeless and all-pervading. This is often called **Consciousness** or the **SELF** or sometimes God, but this term *God* has many meanings ... most that suggest IT is **outside** or *beyond* everything else including this entity called *'me'*. That interpretation would make ONE, *more* than ONE. For absolute clarity, it will not be used in this little book.

ONE cannot experience **IT SELF** without a **frame of reference** and so the **illusion of the universe** is *projected* on the screen of Consciousness [IT SELF] to manifest a **dream-environment** of *more than* ONE. This means this illusion is *inside* IT ... not outside since ONE cannot have an **outside**.

Imagine this projection like Pure Light shining through a prism and producing many colors, yet still the ONE Pure Light. Everything *inside*

ONE is projected into numberless entities from star systems and galaxies in the macrocosm to subatomic particles and waves in the microcosm ... all ONE yet *appearing* as many.

ONE then projects ITs Awareness into each and every one of these illusory entities in order to experience IT SELF. For a season, ONE **forgets** Who IT Really *is* in order to fully *experience* and *savor* the *contrast* this illusion produces.

This projected illusion generates the **appearance** of **separation,** and from this the entire fantasy becomes a *dream* in which ONE **identifies** with each of these separate entities and believes IT **'is'** what IT identifies with. However, the illusion of **separation** and **contrast** also generates the concept of **lack** and **limitation**, which in turn produces **conflict** and a constantly simmering **fear** that rises and falls on a roller coaster called *happiness and sorrow* ... the *inevitable result* of contrast.

From this belief in separation and the **limiting feelings** it generates, the concept of **victims** arises in the entity that is **self aware** called **humanity** [self in this case meaning the false-self-illusion of person-hood]. This occurs due to the belief that in separation there is a scale from lesser to greater ... a **hierarchy** of *'have's and have not's.*

With the belief in victims comes **suffering**. Pain is the counterpart of pleasure in the illusion/dream of separation and is therefore inescapable ... but **suffering** manifests *from* this belief in **victims.**

Nevertheless, **without suffering** the SELF would be **doomed** to forever dream in the illusion IT manifested to experience IT SELF. This then may be referred to as the **Divine Discontent,** which eventually brings the suffering human [false self] to its knees in **surrender** where the SELF [dreaming IT is an individual entity] **experiences a chink-in-the-armor** *of* **the illusion/dream** where IT can begin to focus ITs attention **inward** on IT SELF again.

This **focused attention** ultimately returns ITs **full Awareness** to the **ONE** IT 'is'.

THIS IS THE PROCESS THAT IS
ACCELERATING NOW.

CHAPTER TWO
THE GRAND DREAM

This elaborate projected illusion, in which the SELF experiences IT SELF, may be called the **Grand Dream.**

Since the SELF, while IT sleeps within this dream, believes IT *is* each and every one of the illusory individual entities within it ... each one's experience is, as a result - unique. The unique qualities of each one's dream are sculpted out of their **identifications, expectations and attachments *to*** what is appearing and happening within their individual dream. This is called their *conditioning*.

From this unique template the individual entity called **me** unfolds and is called the **body-mind-identity or person,** also called the **false self.** This ... is the illusory vehicle the **SELF** uses to navigate the **Grand Dream**, tasting contrast and experiencing IT SELF while in the **unconscious** state of the false self [consciousness of the dream as reality *is* unconsciousness of **Truth**]

As stated, while IT dreams within the Grand Dream illusion the SELF believes IT **is** each one of these individuals and from this **ALL** the **stories and dramas** that humanity experiences roll out on the great stage of the world.

NONE OF IT IS REAL ... BECAUSE **WHAT IS REAL** DOES NOT COME AND GO AND HAS NO BEGINNING OR ENDING.

HIGHER POWER

Eventually, there arises the belief in some *higher power* that presides over the tiny activities and experiences of each one's world and from this, over long periods of **time** [an emanation of the illusion of separation] various beliefs manifest that are called **religions**.

Religions manifest from the teachings of the SELF that has fully **freed** IT SELF *from* the illusion of personhood ... often called a master, guru, sage, saint or other Being that has *remembered* Who they Really Are – **ONE**.

Their teachings and example are then **diluted** through the **conditioning** of those who follow that particular liberated version of the SELF and **Truth is mixed with the illusion/dream** thereby manifesting more **dreams** *within* **the Grand Dream.**

NONE OF THESE HAS EVER LED TO LIBERATION BY THEIR FOLLOWERS. HOWEVER, MANY HAVE BEEN LED **THROUGH** THESE BELIEF SYSTEMS, TO THE DEEP INNER SEARCH THAT REMOVES THE BLOCKS TO THE AWARENESS OF THE **SELF.** THIS SEARCH IS CALLED ...

SELF INQUIRY/SURRENDER.

This means that eventually the dreaming version of the SELF must *release* **everything IT has learned** within the Grand Dream and turn within in order for the **Truth of Who IT Really is to be revealed.**

CHAPTER THREE
THE GREAT SHIFT

Within the Grand Dream there are cycles, again from the macrocosm to the microcosm. Some of these cycles are called circadian rhythms that revolve around the body-mind's daily cycles, there are also menstrual cycles, seasonal cycles and galactic cycles and many more. One of these galactic cycles may be called *a Great SHIFT*, which is tied to **the rise and fall of the opposites** that alternatively dominate the illusion of separation.

In our particular sun system this cycle is approximately 26,000 years, half dominated by the **Divine Feminine** influence and half by the **Divine Masculine** influence, each for about 11,000 years with two neutral phases between for about 2,000 years each.

PATRIARCHY AND MATRIARCHY

These two predominate periods are called the **matriarchal** and **patriarchal phases**. A **patriarchal** phase *interfaced* with a **neutral phase** <u>recently</u> and as a result has been *fading* as can be witnessed *everywhere* by **collapsing masculine structures.**

When viewed through the lens of the separated self **[false self]** there is great judgment and finger pointing as ancient abuses, particularly related to the feminine are being *exposed* as they collapse. The SELF however, **knows nothing of judgment** and as the Awareness of the SELF expands, **the Great SHIFT** is recognized as *another great opportunity* for humanity to experience a *mass awakening of Who it Really Is.*

Some few who have already remembered the **SELF** as **Who they Really Are** have remained in a physical body during this **SHIFT** as *examples* of the possibility that awaits **ALL** who have arrived at the moment when the Grand Dream is no longer enough ... when **the urge for Truth** supersedes every possible distraction .

During the Great SHIFT the previously dominating influence [in this case masculine] appears to *expand* like a super nova **just before** exploding ... it struggles and gasps out its last attempt to dominate through what has become a *highly dysfunctional influence*.

LOOK AROUND ... WHAT DO YOU SEE?

Everywhere there are **desperate attempts** by **the dissolving patriarchy** to hold onto its grip of the world dream. This procession into the **neutral phase** includes the advent of *mass communication*, literally available to almost everyone so that **what has been easily hidden** from humanity for eons [time also being an illusion] **is now openly and instantly available.**

This means that the **clandestine activities** that once controlled every aspect of the world dream no longer have an **exclusive** influence on how the dream plays out. However, there is a **great struggle** within these SHIFT years and as a result *a steep rise in fear and suffering.*

The intensity of this struggle increases to such a point that **much of humanity** is being brought to the *breaking point* where the allure of the dream can no longer hold undivided attention.

Some will leave the body only to return to another body for additional attempts to **Free** themselves from the dream of separation ... these returns are more **dreams within the Grand Dream**. Others will fall to their knees in desperation and cry out for help, **attempting to bargain** with some so-called higher power to release them from the **fiery transition** of the SHIFT.

Some of these ones however [**many** compared to historical numbers] will, in *deep sincerity* cry out for Help to find a **better way** and it is in this **sustained sincerity** that the turn within occurs as the fully Conscious SELF **always responds** to the *genuine and humble attention* given to IT by the slumbering SELF [IT also Is] within the Grand Dream.

CHAPTER FOUR
WHAT'S REALLY HAPPENING

WHATEVER AND HOWEVER THESE **DRAMATIC STORIES** PLAY OUT ON THE WORLD STAGE WITHIN THE GRAND DREAM AS THE GREAT SHIFT EXPANDS ... **ARE OF LITTLE SIGNIFICANCE.**

They just happen to be the **current dream instruments** through which **the Great SHIFT is** flowing to bring about the *mass awakening opportunity now unfolding.*

Most of humanity still sleeps deeply within the dream and as a result most of its attention is given to **the body's welfare** as it relates to these stories and dramas. This means **current events receive the highest priority** and it is because of this, that through the influence *thought* has on the *mouldable substance* of the dream, remaining asleep continues as more and more dreams are produced ... what the false self refers to as *creating your own reality.*

NOTHING COULD BE FURTHER FROM THE TRUTH, SINCE THERE IS ONLY **ONE REALITY – THE SELF,** AND IT NEVER CHANGES.

What thought really does is simply **manifest more dreams**, something that is heavily touted as very desirable, but which actually takes the slumbering SELF, in its false self illusion - deeper into the Grand Dream.

It is only when attention is **funneled down to a point** that *focuses WITHIN* that the SELF can radiate the Truth *of* IT SELF *to* the sleeping aspect *of* IT SELF wrapped tightly as IT is, within **the veils of conditioning called the false self or person.**

THE VALUE OF SUFFERING
Suffering is always the first influence that tends to **narrow attention. As suffering**

intensifies there is an **outreach** toward *where* the false self believes **help** may be available.

This begins with the many **ways and means** available within the dream such as **religions, philosophies, psychologies, medicines, therapies and counseling** depending on what kind of suffering is happening. These modalities may have **some temporary effect** and for a period the suffering may reduce or even cease.

This may last throughout one's entire lifetime until the end of the body, which *guarantees* that **the sleeping SELF** will **return** in another dream body-mind-identity for another opportunity to **discover IT SELF** from behind the clouds of illusion that ITs conditioning has manifested.

Some few reach a point where they **can no longer endure the suffering** and where outside assistance fails to alleviate it. It is at this **line-in-the-sand** where **True *Surrender*** occurs and the choice to be **Free NO MATTER WHAT** places the sleeping SELF on *the fast-track HOME to Self Realization.*

Very few have arrived at this point and gone on to **recognize** Who They Really Are and thereby return permanently to the **full Awareness** of the **ONE SELF**. Many have experienced **moments of intense Light,** often referred to *as satori's, epiphanies or AHA's,* but have not **sustained the Light** long enough to transform ALL the conditioning that bound them to the belief in separation as **the illusion of an individual person.**

The imbalanced influence of the **patriarchy or matriarchy**, depending on which was dominating, generated enormous **conflict and chaos** since the original so-called **fall of man**, the religious Garden of Eden fantasy, which actually describes the **Fall of Consciousness** from ITs **SELF Awareness as ONE.**

These **dysfunctional and imbalanced environments** that unfold in either the matriarchal or patriarchal phases make it extremely difficult for even the most ardent aspirant to reclaim the *full Awareness of the SELF* as **Who They Really Are.**

However, when the Grand Dream **SHIFTS** into these 2,000 year neutral phases [still a dream within the Grand Dream], the opportunity to **return to this Awareness increases exponentially**. And, as said,

THIS IS *PRECEDED BY* THE COLLAPSE OF THE PREVIOUSLY DOMINATING INFLUENCE ...

IN THIS CASE A **PATRIARCHY** AND A BRIEF PERIOD OF **HIGHLY ELEVATED CHAOS**, WHICH THE WORLD AND HUMANITY *IS NOW EXPERIENCING.*

This magnified chaos in turn **increases global suffering** and brings many to this line-in-the-sand stage where genuine **Surrender** occurs.

THIS ... **is what is now occurring** and is an *enormous blessing*, which will ... for many, lead to **Freedom**.

CHAPTER FIVE
THE TURN WITHIN - NAVIGATING THE GREAT SHIFT

*"Whatever is destined **not to happen** will not happen, try as you may. Whatever is destined **to** happen **will happen,** do what you may to prevent it. This is certain. The best course, therefore, is to remain **silent**."* - **Ramana**

Silence in this context does not necessarily mean the absence of sound, [although that **can be** the case] ... it means *mind activity* ceases. As stated, the mind [body-mind-identity] *is an illusion* and nothing that emanates **from it is True**, no matter how beautiful it may seem.

It is the mind's activity that **magnifies** and **perpetuates** the *conditioning* that makes up the **fictional person** most believe they are, as well as the **world/universe they experience**.

ITS ALL *MAKE-BELIEVE*.

When there is **conflict and chaos** ... [*and there is always conflict and chaos on some level because the dream is produced out of the belief in separation*], the mind **resists** and **attempts to handle or control** events. Within the dream the mind manifested, thought *expands* circumstances depending on the degree of *attention and passion* that is given to any **focus.**

This is why, when the mind **resists** it is **giving life TO** whatever it wants to control and/or **get-rid-of** with the result being ... an **expansion of** that very situation.

Despite the widespread awareness that *thoughts create experience*, this process of **shooting-one's-self-in-the-foot** scenario persists ... *remembering that this experience is still ... just a dream.*

During **major change** within the Grand Dream ... such as **_now_** during **_the Great SHIFT,_** there is a **_massive knee-jerk-reaction_** by the mind [individually as well as by the bulk of humanity] to resist **far more passionately** than with what may be called - **normal challenges.**

This **_rushes oxygen to the fire_** of chaos and produces **_stampeding fear._** This fear is then **easily manipulated _by those who dominate,_** as is evidenced by current world conditions, and is the chief instrument in the last-ditch attempts by the collapsing patriarchy to try to maintain its **control** over humanity.

As said earlier, the world has been experienced **_upside-down_** since the **Fall of Consciousness** while **the mind [the false self] has dominated.** The **SELF**, the ONE Consciousness YOU Really Are, functions totally differently than the illusory mind.

When you **_surrender to the SELF_**, the world does not suddenly become Peaceful as many spiritual belief systems proclaim, because there is a **momentum** present. Its like when you are driving a car and take your foot off the accelerator … there will still be forward motion until the lack of energy **[attention]** drains the life from the movement, and the car **[circumstance]** stops.

The **SELF is Peace IT SELF** and *need do nothing* for Peace to exist. When your attention is placed *on* Peace [for example], you are allowing *What IS to simply BE.* You are not attempting to **think or act Peace into existence**, rather you are simply **experiencing IT** as **Your True SELF.** This is effortless and this is why when one returns to the **full Awareness of the SELF** or ONE They Are, they *Live IN the world but not OF the world.*

The conflict and chaos is still there but **their experience** is that of Peace … its like being in the eye of a storm. This Peace may be referred to as **Love** or **Beauty** or **Freedom** or many other words for Truth. In this *True state* they are **not adding fuel to the fire** by giving

attention to the momentum of the fire. They are giving their **attention** to Truth and so their world experience **expands in Truth.**

This is why the SELF is often referred to as: *The Light of the World.*

During the Great SHIFT this **stampeding fear** and **mass manipulation WILL** increase temporarily, and this will **expand global suffering.** It will seem for a while that the patriarchy is indeed taking over the world, but it's the **last gasp** of the end of an 11,000 year dysfunctional patriarchal cycle.

While this **last burst of control** persists, the **breaking point** mentioned earlier will be reached by many and this will bring them to their knees in *genuine* **surrender.** This is the *enormous blessing* of this transition **out of** this **patriarchal phase** and **into** a *neutral phase* where *a degree of balance reigns* for about 2,000 years of clock time ... *still, remembering it is just a dream.*

At first there is this **knee-jerk-reaction** but ultimately **surrender** ensues. For many, this surrender will be **sincere** and **continuous.** As a result, their **reunion** with the **Voice of Silence** [the SELF] will begin to occur leading them deeper and deeper within where their **Attention** will be **totally on the SELF** [by whatever name they use – Love, Peace, Beauty, Freedom, I AM, etc].

HOW TO NAVIGATE THE SHIFT

The simplest way to approach this *reunion* with the Real YOU [the SELF] is to *say YES to What IS.* This does not mean you are agreeing with the prevailing conflict and chaos … it means that **you are NOT resisting it.** *THIS … is True Surrender.*

The events now unfolding on the **world stage** are *inevitable* and *predestined* based on the conditioning each one came in with and are manifesting **as** the Great SHIFT … of this, **there is no choice.** The one choice you **DO** have is to this **YES to What IS,** which is your **surrender** to

Truth, allowing IT to *take over your life experience completely.*

THIS IS THE **SIMPLE** WAY TO NAVIGATE THE GREAT SHIFT.

If you attempt to **resist what is unfolding** your transition through the Great SHIFT will be far more dramatic and fiery … however, each one comes to the line-in-the-sand in their own way **where they can take no more**.

Nevertheless, take heart … **ALL IS WELL.** As the great sage Ramana said:

"WHATEVER IS DESTINED TO HAPPEN WILL HAPPEN…"

AND THIS MEANS ALL WILL EVENTUALLY RETURN TO THE FULL AWARENESS OF THE SELF THEY ARE.

ABOUT THE AUTHOR

John McIntosh

A Multi-millionaire until 1999 John traveled for decades around the world speaking to tens of thousands of people before leaving everything behind and surrendering totally to the SELF. John shares his experience as a successful entrepreneur, fulfilling his every dream and then dropping that mask for the True experience of the SELF We All Are.

LINKS

BOOKS by John McIntosh

https://www.johnmcintosh.info/copy-of-books

SUBSCRIBE to John McIntosh's daily BLOG

https://www.johnmcintosh.info/subscribe

SELF INQUIRY - eBook

https://www.amazon.com/dp/B07YKCHFP3

TESTIMONIALS

An AMAZON #1 New Release [in 45-Minute Self-Help Short Reads]

I've been reading spiritual books for decades. I've read most of the best authors, but none has been as clear as John's books. - Rod Spain

John writes from his Heart with such incredible inspirational power. - Wendy Embleton Huber

You are as clear and direct a teacher as I've come across - Alex Alioto

Amazing writing. I feel it in my Heart. - Irina Isakov

Such clarity and simplicity in your ability to communicate the Truth. Christine Van Hoose

CPSIA information can be obtained
at www.ICGtesting.com
Printed in the USA
BVHW011418150922
647141BV00007B/333